WHY DON'T COUNTRY FLAGS USE THE COLOR PURPLE?

by
AFTER SKOOL

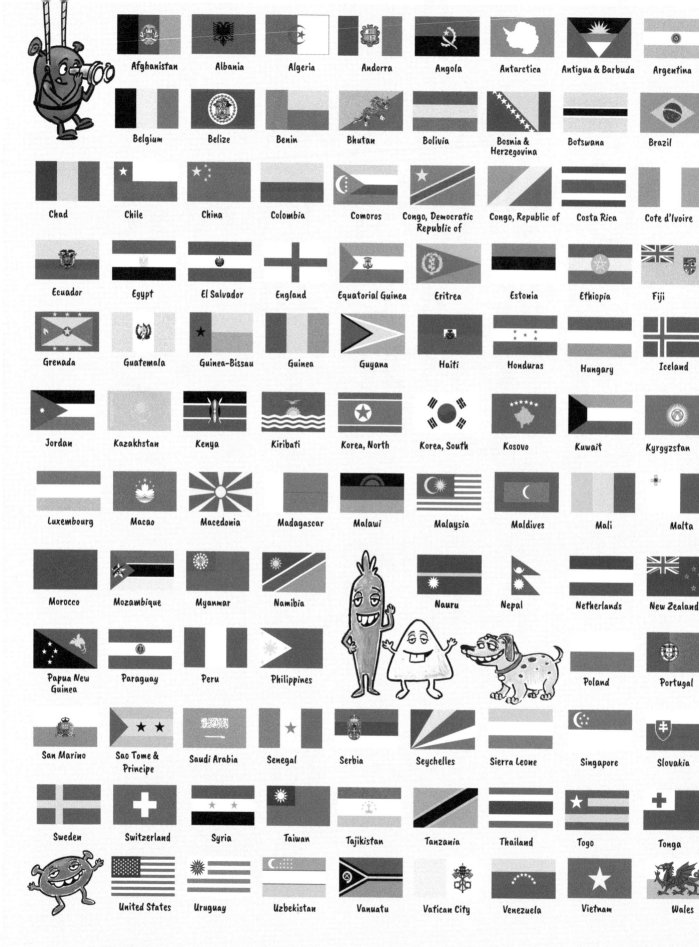

| Afghanistan | Albania | Algeria | Andorra | Angola | Antarctica | Antigua & Barbuda | Argentina |

| Belgium | Belize | Benin | Bhutan | Bolivia | Bosnia & Herzegovina | Botswana | Brazil |

| Chad | Chile | China | Colombia | Comoros | Congo, Democratic Republic of | Congo, Republic of | Costa Rica | Cote d'Ivoire |

| Ecuador | Egypt | El Salvador | England | Equatorial Guinea | Eritrea | Estonia | Ethiopia | Fiji |

| Grenada | Guatemala | Guinea-Bissau | Guinea | Guyana | Haiti | Honduras | Hungary | Iceland |

| Jordan | Kazakhstan | Kenya | Kiribati | Korea, North | Korea, South | Kosovo | Kuwait | Kyrgyzstan |

| Luxembourg | Macao | Macedonia | Madagascar | Malawi | Malaysia | Maldives | Mali | Malta |

| Morocco | Mozambique | Myanmar | Namibia | Nauru | Nepal | Netherlands | New Zealand |

| Papua New Guinea | Paraguay | Peru | Philippines | Poland | Portugal |

| San Marino | Sao Tome & Principe | Saudi Arabia | Senegal | Serbia | Seychelles | Sierra Leone | Singapore | Slovakia |

| Sweden | Switzerland | Syria | Taiwan | Tajikistan | Tanzania | Thailand | Togo | Tonga |

| United States | Uruguay | Uzbekistan | Vanuatu | Vatican City | Venezuela | Vietnam | Wales |

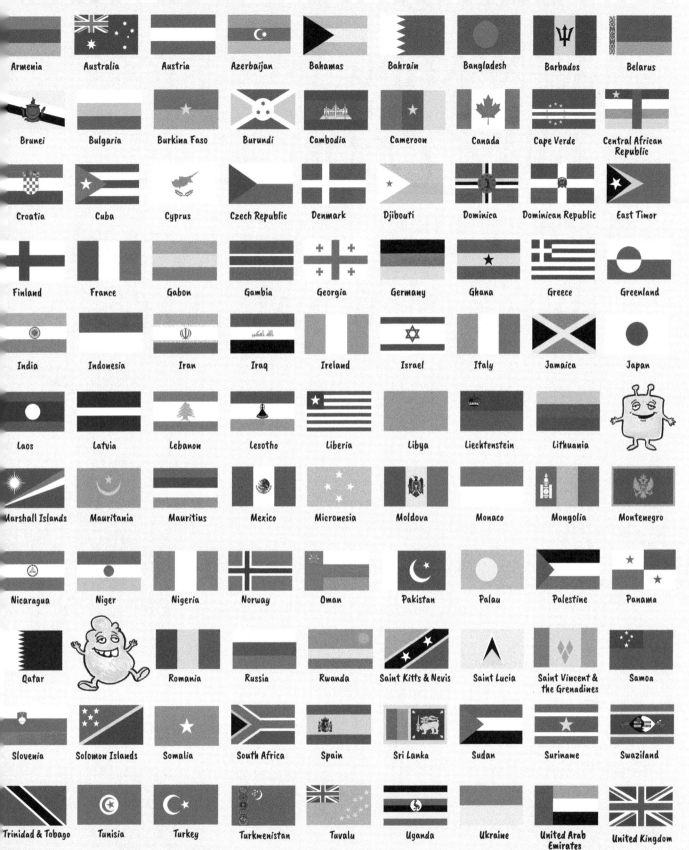

Armenia	Australia	Austria	Azerbaijan
Bahamas	Bahrain	Bangladesh	Barbados	Belarus
Brunei	Bulgaria	Burkina Faso	Burundi	Cambodia	Cameroon	Canada	Cape Verde	Central African Republic
Croatia	Cuba	Cyprus	Czech Republic	Denmark	Djibouti	Dominica	Dominican Republic	East Timor
Finland	France	Gabon	Gambia	Georgia	Germany	Ghana	Greece	Greenland
India	Indonesia	Iran	Iraq	Ireland	Israel	Italy	Jamaica	Japan
Laos	Latvia	Lebanon	Lesotho	Liberia	Libya	Liechtenstein	Lithuania	
Marshall Islands	Mauritania	Mauritius	Mexico	Micronesia	Moldova	Monaco	Mongolia	Montenegro
Nicaragua	Niger	Nigeria	Norway	Oman	Pakistan	Palau	Palestine	Panama
Qatar		Romania	Russia	Rwanda	Saint Kitts & Nevis	Saint Lucia	Saint Vincent & the Grenadines	Samoa
Slovenia	Solomon Islands	Somalia	South Africa	Spain	Sri Lanka	Sudan	Suriname	Swaziland
Trinidad & Tobago	Tunisia	Turkey	Turkmenistan	Tuvalu	Uganda	Ukraine	United Arab Emirates	United Kingdom
Yemen	Zambia	Zimbabwe						

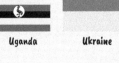

THE AMAZING TRUE STORY OF WHY COUNTRIES DON'T USE PURPLE ON THEIR NATIONAL FLAGS

Hello Class, Welcome to After Skool!
I'm Professor Q.
Today we're going to learn about COUNTRY FLAGS.
There are 196 countries on earth and every
single one has a flag.

I SEE GREEN
I SPOT ORANGE
THERE'S RED
WOO HOO BLUE
WHERE'S PURPLE?

Hold on! Hold on! Stop teasing Purple! There's actually a very special reason why countries don't use purple on their flags.

Let's go on a journey through history!

The reason why we don't see purple on country flags is because it was TOO EXPENSIVE! For thousands of years, purple dye was worth more than silver, gold or diamonds!

Purple was so precious because there was only one place on earth where purple fabric could be dyed.
This was in the trading city of Tyre, which is in modern day Lebanon.

The special dye used to color purple fabric came from a rare sea snail.

And this sea snail was ONLY found in the ocean by the city of Tyre. So the bright purple color was known throughout the world as "Tyrian purple".

Finding the purple dye was dangerous work.
Divers had to swim deep into the ocean
to collect drops of slimy snot from
each snail.

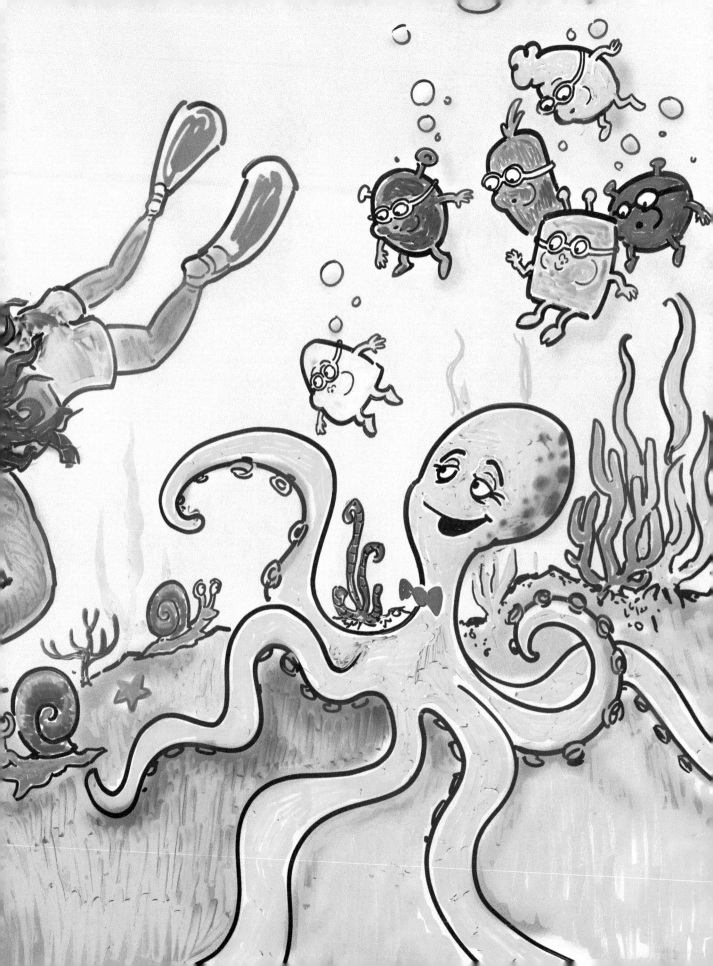

Believe it or not, it would take 10,000 snails to make 1 gram of Tyrian purple dye! It could take over 1 million snails to color a single royal robe! TRUE STORY!

1 GRAM

So why not
just mix red and blue dye
to make purple dye?
Wouldn't that be easier
than collecting all those
snails?

Great question! However, hundreds of years ago dyeing clothes was not so simple. Old fabric dyes were made from flowers, leaves or berries. These dyes did not mix well or last long. They would fade in the sun or wash away in water.

Tyrian purple was so special because it was the brightest, most beautiful shade of purple. It never faded or washed away. No other fabric could match the brilliance of true Tyrian Purple!

Tyrian Purple

Mixing blue and red

Since only wealthy rulers could afford to buy and wear Tyrian purple, it became associated with the royal families of Rome, Egypt, and Persia.

Common folks suffered serious punishment if they were caught wearing any Tyrian purple!

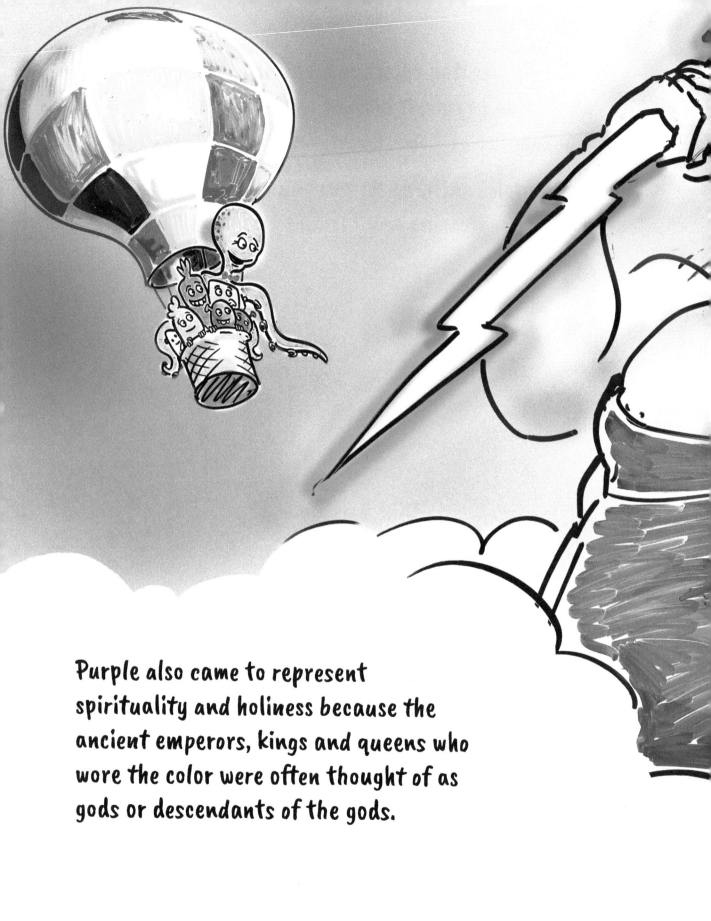

Purple also came to represent
spirituality and holiness because the
ancient emperors, kings and queens who
wore the color were often thought of as
gods or descendants of the gods.

So since the price of purple was so ridiculously high, no one, not even the richest nations, could afford to have purple on their flag.

But everything changed in the year 1856.
An 18 year old chemist named William Henry Perkin
set out to find a cure for malaria, a deadly
disease spread by mosquitoes. In his attempt to
discover new medicine, William accidently created
something entirely
different...

William noticed that his failed science experiment could be used to dye fabrics. He took his invention and built a huge purple dyeing factory! This discovery would completely change the fashion world.

In fact, many of the greatest scientific breakthroughs were discovered by accident!

Purple dye was then mass produced so just about everybody in the world could wear it.

No more snails were needed to make bright purple fabric.

Kings and queens stopped valuing purple and the status symbol faded away, but the country flags remain the same...

DOMINICA

Since the year 1900, a handful of new national flags have been designed and the tiny country of Dominica decided to put a purple parrot on their flag! So there is one!

In Conclusion:

Something that was precious 150 years ago is now cheap and abundant. Perhaps things we consider valuable today, like gold or oil, will become worthless in the future.

And vice versa, what things do we take for granted that may one day become precious? Water? Oxygen? Maybe YOU will be the next great inventor who changes the world...

ISBN 978-0-578-48924-7

The text of this book is typeset in Caveat Brush

After Skool started as an animation channel on YouTube.
The goal was to create videos that enhance life-changing ideas,
most of which are not taught in a classroom. This book is based
on one of our most popular videos.

If you'd like to see more art and learn about some fun topics,
please visit our YouTube channel. We specialize in taking complex
content and simplifying it into entertaining, bite-size pieces.
Some people learn by reading, some learn by listening, some by
seeing and others by doing. We combine all learning styles to
make education effortless and fun!

YouTube.com/c/AfterSkool

This book was illustrated by
Mark W.

This is the trading city of Tyre that was located in Phoenicia, what is now the coastal region of Lebanon. The first Tyrian purple fabric was dyed here in 1570 BC. Phoenician meant 'purple people' in ancient Greek.

In Phoenician mythology, Tyrian purple was discovered when a pet dog bit into a sea snail that washed ashore

Tyrian purple dye comes from the mucus glands of the predatory sea snail known as the Murex

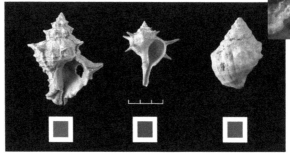

The Murex's Latin name is purpura, which is where we got the word purple from.

Julius Caesar was the first to wear an all purple toga in 50 BC.

Roman generals were permitted to wear purple after winning a major battle

Sometimes the dye was too expensive even for royalty. 3rd century Roman Emperor, Aurelian famously wouldn't allow his wife to buy a shawl made from Tyrian purple because it was too expensive

This mosaic shows Justinian The Great, emperor of the Byzantine Empire from 527 - 565 AD. This is one of the oldest art examples of royalty wearing Tyrian purple.

Purple also represented wealth and royalty in Japan.

1 pound of Tyrian purple dye used to cost as much as 3 pounds of gold, which is worth over $60,000 USD in 2019.

The term "born in purple" referred to someone of royal or high class.

St Edward's Crown, crafted in 1660, is the oldest existing and most famous English crown.

In England, Queen Elizabeth I forbade anyone outside of the royal family to wear purple during her reign from 1558 - 1603. Violators could be tortured or even sentenced to death.

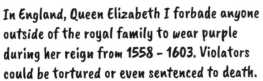

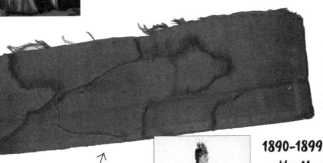

Perkin's Purple.

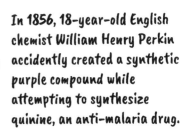

his is one of the first pieces f fabric that William Henry erkin dyed. He patented his vention in 1856 and called "Mauve".

1890-1899 was known as the Mauve Decade because people could access purple clothes for the first time.

In 1856, 18-year-old English chemist William Henry Perkin accidentally created a synthetic purple compound while attempting to synthesize quinine, an anti-malaria drug.

The Second Spanish Republic, which formed in 1931, also used purple on its flag, but the country fell apart only 8 years later in 1939.

Purple Heart medal given to U.S. military members who were wounded in battle.

Purple is the rarest color in nature and it is the hardest for our eyes to see.

Even today, purple still holds historic and symbolic meaning for royalty. Queen Elizabeth II is commonly seen in all purple.

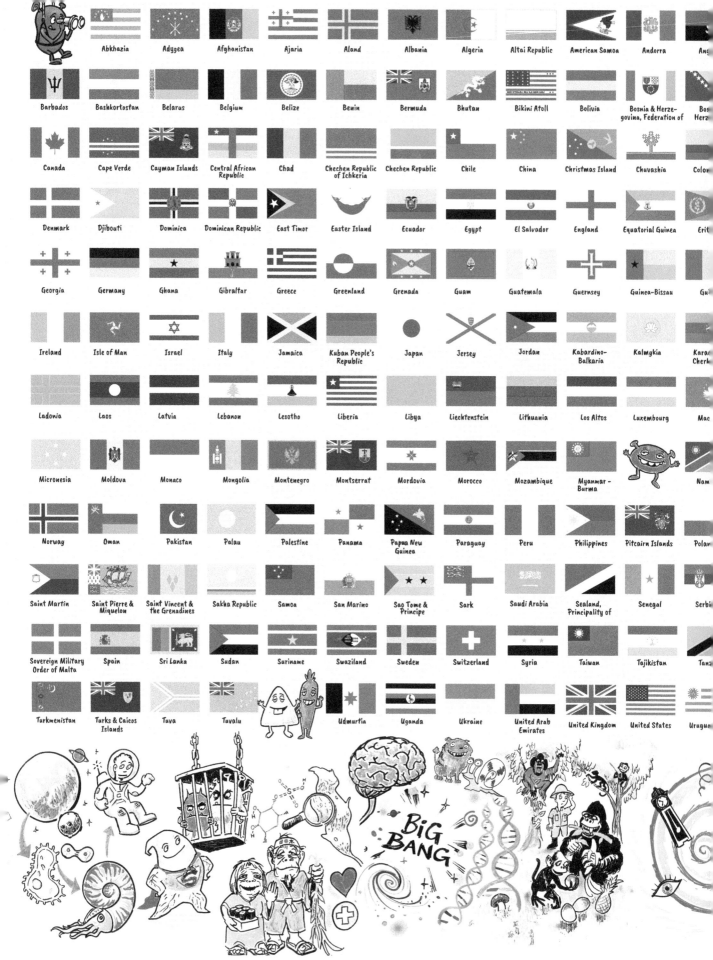

Abkhazia | Adygea | Afghanistan | Ajaria | Aland | Albania | Algeria | Altai Republic | American Samoa | Andorra | Ang

Barbados | Bashkortostan | Belarus | Belgium | Belize | Benin | Bermuda | Bhutan | Bikini Atoll | Bolivia | Bosnia & Herzegovina, Federation of | Bos Herz

Canada | Cape Verde | Cayman Islands | Central African Republic | Chad | Chechen Republic of Ichkeria | Chechen Republic | Chile | China | Christmas Island | Chuvashia | Color

Denmark | Djibouti | Dominica | Dominican Republic | East Timor | Easter Island | Ecuador | Egypt | El Salvador | England | Equatorial Guinea | Erit

Georgia | Germany | Ghana | Gibraltar | Greece | Greenland | Grenada | Guam | Guatemala | Guernsey | Guinea-Bissau | Gu

Ireland | Isle of Man | Israel | Italy | Jamaica | Kuban People's Republic | Japan | Jersey | Jordan | Kabardino-Balkaria | Kalmykia | Karar Cherk

Ladonia | Laos | Latvia | Lebanon | Lesotho | Liberia | Libya | Liechtenstein | Lithuania | Los Altos | Luxembourg | Mac

Micronesia | Moldova | Monaco | Mongolia | Montenegro | Montserrat | Mordovia | Morocco | Mozambique | Myanmar – Burma | Nam

Norway | Oman | Pakistan | Palau | Palestine | Panama | Papua New Guinea | Paraguay | Peru | Philippines | Pitcairn Islands | Polan

Saint Martin | Saint Pierre & Miquelon | Saint Vincent & the Grenadines | Sakha Republic | Samoa | San Marino | Sao Tome & Principe | Sark | Saudi Arabia | Sealand, Principality of | Senegal | Serbi

Sovereign Military Order of Malta | Spain | Sri Lanka | Sudan | Suriname | Swaziland | Sweden | Switzerland | Syria | Taiwan | Tajikistan | Tanz

Turkmenistan | Turks & Caicos Islands | Tuva | Tuvalu | Udmurtia | Uganda | Ukraine | United Arab Emirates | United Kingdom | United States | Urugue

BIG BANG

guilla	Antarctica	Antigua & Barbuda	Argentina	Armenia	Aruba	Australia	Austria	Azerbaijan	Bahamas	Bahrain	Bangladesh
swana	Brazil	British Antarctic Territory	British Indian Ocean Territory	Brittany	Brunei	Bulgaria	Burkina Faso	Burundi	Buryatia	Cambodia	Cameroon
moros	Congo Democratic Republic of the	Congo, Republic of the	Cook Islands	Costa Rica	Cote d'Ivoire	Crimea	Croatia	Cuba	Cyprus	Czech Republic	Dagestan
tonia	Ethiopia	Falkland Islands	Faroe Islands	Fiji	Finland	France	French Polynesia	French Southern & Antarctic Lands	Gabon	Gambia	
yana	Haiti	Herm	Honduras	Hong Kong	Hungary	Iceland	India	Indonesia	Ingushetia	Iran	Iraq
akalpakstan	Karelia	Kazakhstan	Kenya	Khakassia	Kiribati	Komi	Korea, North	Korea, South	Kosovo	Kuwait	Kyrgyzstan
cedonia	Madagascar	Malawi	Malaysia	Maldives	Mali	Malta	Mari El	Marshall Islands	Mauritania	Mauritius	Mexico
auru	Nepal	Netherlands Antilles	Netherlands	New Zealand	Nicaragua	Niger	Nigeria	Niue	Norfolk Island	North Ossetia	Northern Mariana Islands
rtugal	Puerto Rico	Qatar	Republika Srpska	Romania	Russia	Rwanda	Saba	Saint Barthelemy	Saint Helena	Saint Kitts & Nevis	Saint Lucia
eychelles	Sierra Leone	Sikkim	Singapore	Slovakia	Slovenia	Solomon Islands	Somalia	Somaliland	South Africa	South Georgia & the South Sandwich Islands	South Ossetia
atarstan	Thailand		Togo	Tokelau	Tonga	Transnistria	Trinidad & Tobago	Tistan da Cunha	Tunisia	Turkey	Turkish Republic Northern Cyprus
bekistan	Vanuatu	Vatican City	Venezuela	Vietnam	Virgin Islands-UK	Virgin Islands-US	Wales	Western Sahara	Yemen	Zambia	Zimbabwe

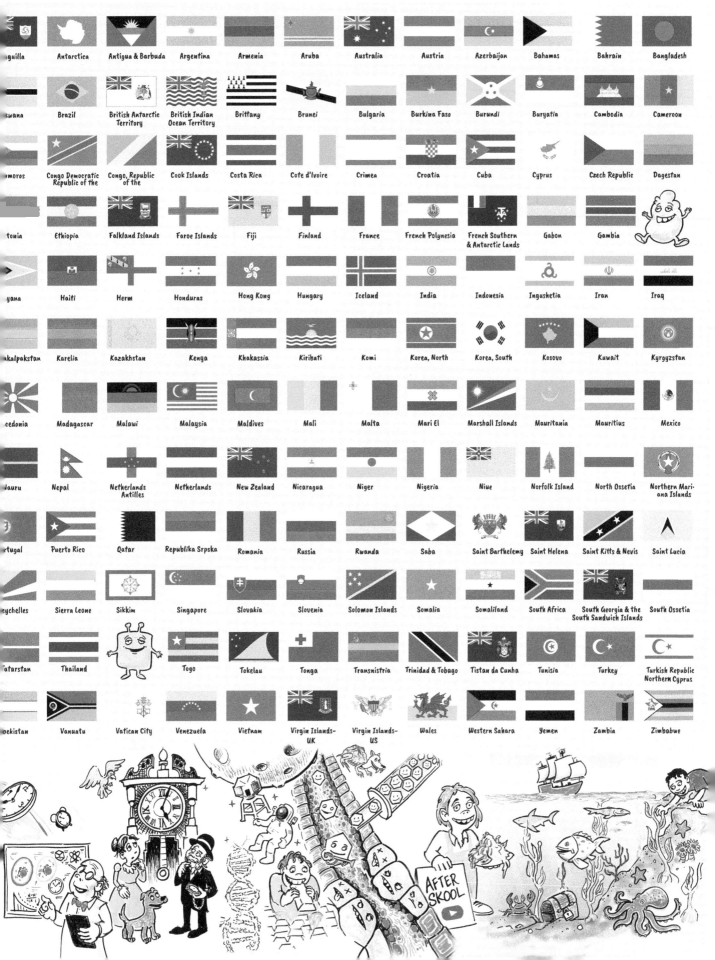

CPSIA information can be obtained
at www.ICGtesting.com
Printed in the USA
LVHW071359030821
694426LV00006B/272